$.95

Classic Border Designs by Twentieth-Century Masters

Bradley, Teague, Cleland, Rogers and Hornung

Edited by
CLARENCE P. HORNUNG

DOVER PUBLICATIONS, INC.
New York

Published in Canada by General Publishing Company, Ltd., 30 Lesmill Road, Don Mills, Toronto, Ontario.
Published in the United Kingdom by Constable and Company, Ltd., 3 The Lanchesters, 162–164 Fulham Palace Road, London W6 9ER.

Bibliographical Note

Classic Border Designs by Twentieth-Century Masters: Bradley, Teague, Cleland, Rogers and Hornung is a new work, first published by Dover Publications, Inc., in 1995.

DOVER *Pictorial Archive* SERIES

Library of Congress Cataloging-in-Publication Data

Classic border designs by twentieth-century masters : Bradley, Teague, Cleland, Rogers, and Hornung / edited by Clarence P. Hornung.
    p.   cm. — (Dover pictorial archive)
  ISBN 0-486-28518-9 (pbk.)
    1. Borders, Ornamental (Decorative arts)—United States—History—20th century—Themes, motives. I. Hornung, Clarence Pearson. II. Series: Dover pictorial archive series.
NK1404.C63 1995
745.4—dc20   95-14867
                                                                              CIP

Manufactured in the United States of America
Dover Publications, Inc., 31 East 2nd Street, Mineola, N.Y. 11501

NOTE

IN THE LATE nineteenth century, with the Arts and Crafts Movement and the establishment of William Morris' Kelmscott Press in England, a renewed sense of artistry emerged in the printing industry. In America, this impetus was the product of individual artists' visions for their craft. The work of five of these artists is collected here, selected and arranged by one of the twentieth-century masters himself, Clarence P. Hornung.

Each of these artists saw the vast possibilities for creative design in printed matter, and each produced a wide range of artistic expression through commercial media: book design and layout, typography and advertising. Will Bradley (1868–1962) began his career as a printer's devil and by 1907 he was art editor of *Collier's Magazine;* over the next several years—already a legendary figure in the printing industry—he was art supervisor of the Hearst publishing empire. Bruce Rogers (1870–1957) was another highly influential book designer/ typographer. Among the more than 400 fine books and limited editions he designed and illustrated are the Oxford Lectern Bible (1935), various works by Shakespeare and other classics, such as *Aesop's Fables* (1933) and *The Rime of the Ancient Mariner* (1930). Influenced by Morris and Bradley, Thomas Maitland Cleland (1880–1964) spent his early career printing books on his own press, set up in his father's cellar. Though the volumes he printed, such as Tennyson's *Lady of Shalott*, were artistically promising, his private venture did not succeed. Cleland assumed the art editorship of *McClure's Magazine* around 1907–08, and in 1914 his association with the Locomobile automobile firm began, ushering in a new phase of American advertising. Walter Dorwin Teague (1883–1960) found fame through advertising as well. Perhaps his most famous designs were created for Arrow Collars. The product of an intense advertising campaign, the "Arrow Collar Man" (whose portrait was created by John C. Leyendecker and embellished with Teague's elaborate and finely drawn borders) was an American phenomenon. By the 1920s the Arrow Man—a fictitious creation—had received 17,000 fan letters, gifts and marriage proposals. Clarence P. Hornung also helped elevate commercial design to new heights. His ornate borders and illustrations, rendered in a variety of styles ranging from Rococo to Art Deco, appeared in such widely circulating magazines as *Life* and *Ladies' Home Journal*, and embellished ads for Locomobile, Howard Watches and New York Central's Twentieth Century Limited commuter train.

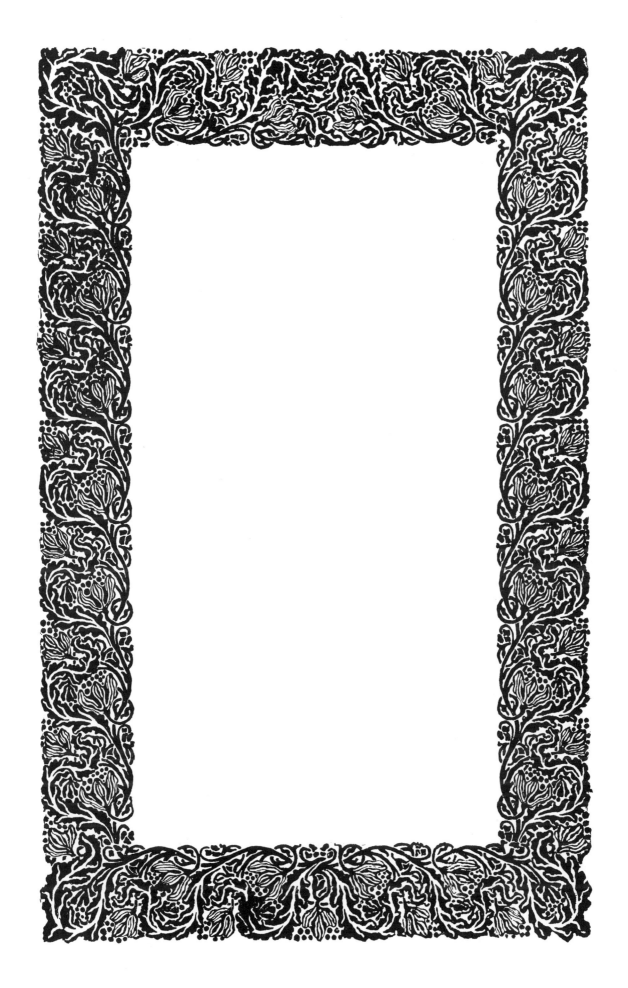

WILL BRADLEY, *1897*

2

WILL BRADLEY, *1896*

WILL BRADLEY, c. *1902*

4   WILL BRADLEY, *1896*

6

WILL BRADLEY, *1895*

7

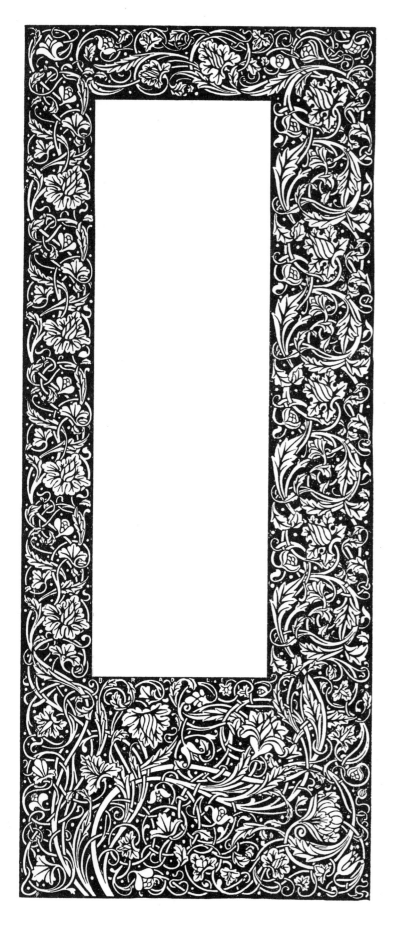

8

WILL BRADLEY, *1896*

WILL BRADLEY, *1896*

10   WILL BRADLEY, *1895*

WILL BRADLEY, *1895*

12   WILL BRADLEY, *1900*

WILL BRADLEY, *1895*

14　　　　　　　　　　WILL BRADLEY, *1905*

WILL BRADLEY, *1895*

16   WILL BRADLEY, *1895*

WILL BRADLEY, *1893*

WALTER DORWIN TEAGUE, *1924*

WALTER DORWIN TEAGUE, *1915*

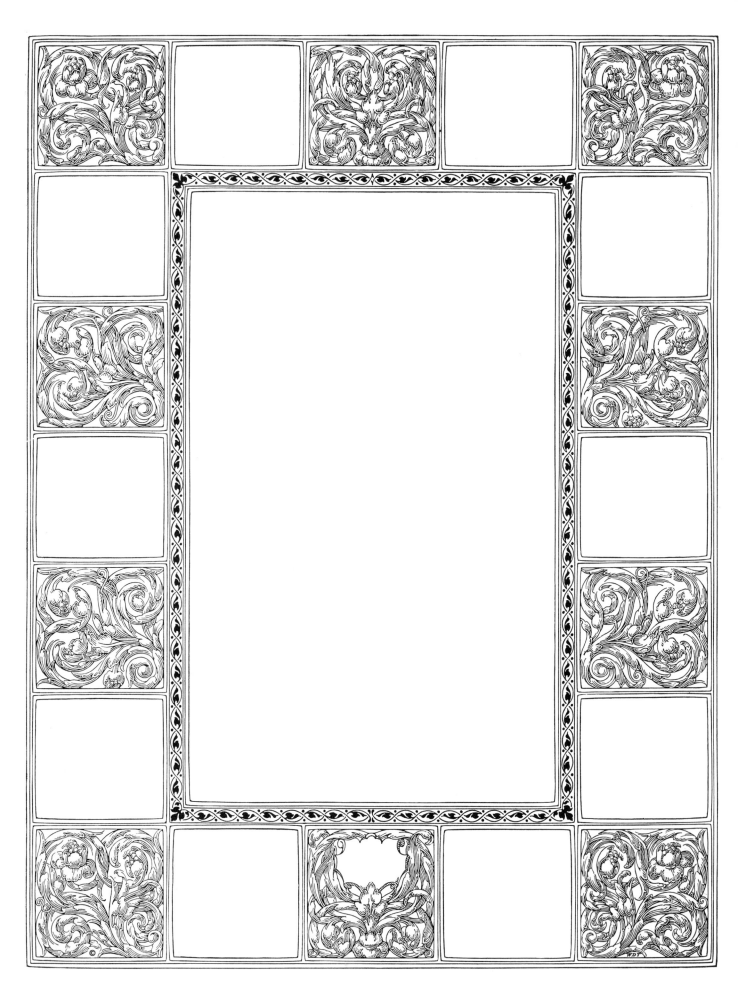

20　　　　　　　　　　　　Walter Dorwin Teague, *1925*

WALTER DORWIN TEAGUE, *1925*

WALTER DORWIN TEAGUE, *1923*

WALTER DORWIN TEAGUE, *1922*

24 WALTER DORWIN TEAGUE, *1923*

WALTER DORWIN TEAGUE, *1920*

WALTER DORWIN TEAGUE, *1924*

WALTER DORWIN TEAGUE, *1925*

Walter Dorwin Teague, *1924*

WALTER DORWIN TEAGUE, *1925*

WALTER DORWIN TEAGUE, *1925*

WALTER DORWIN TEAGUE, *1925*

WALTER DORWIN TEAGUE, *1924*

WALTER DORWIN TEAGUE, *1924*

34   WALTER DORWIN TEAGUE, *1923*

WALTER DORWIN TEAGUE, *1924*

WALTER DORWIN TEAGUE, *1924*

WALTER DORWIN TEAGUE, *1924*

WALTER DORWIN TEAGUE, *1921*

Walter Dorwin Teague, *1920*

WALTER DORWIN TEAGUE, *1919*

42   WALTER DORWIN TEAGUE, *1920*

WALTER DORWIN TEAGUE, *1920*

43

44   WALTER DORWIN TEAGUE, *1919*

WALTER DORWIN TEAGUE, *1917*

Walter Dorwin Teague, *1915*

WALTER DORWIN TEAGUE, *1915*

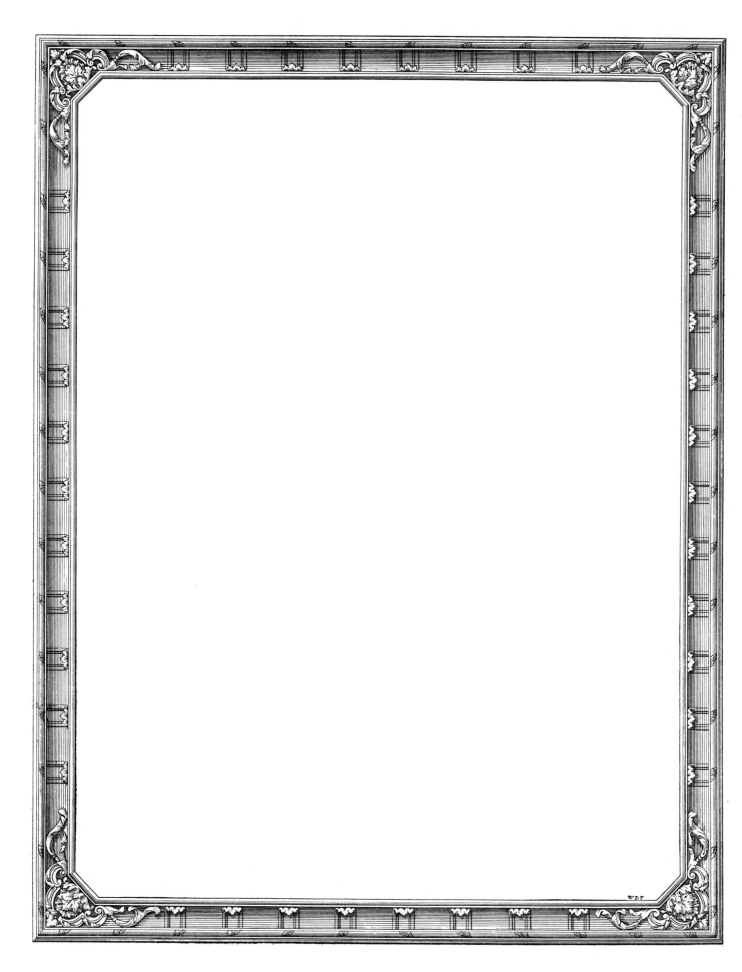

48

WALTER DORWIN TEAGUE, *1917*

T. M. Cleland, *1916*

T. M. CLELAND, *1917 (top); n.d. (bottom)*

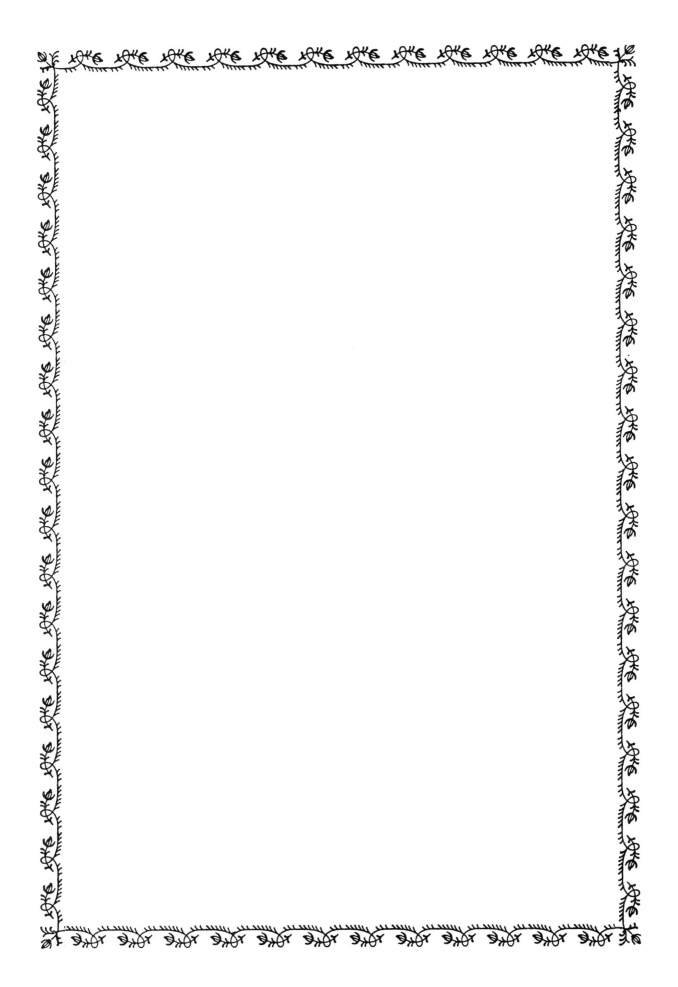

T. M. CLELAND, *c. 1920*

54   T. M. Cleland, *1917*

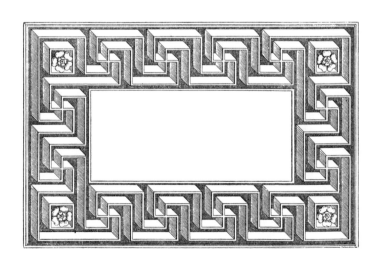

T. M. Cleland, *1921*

T. M. CLELAND, *1910*

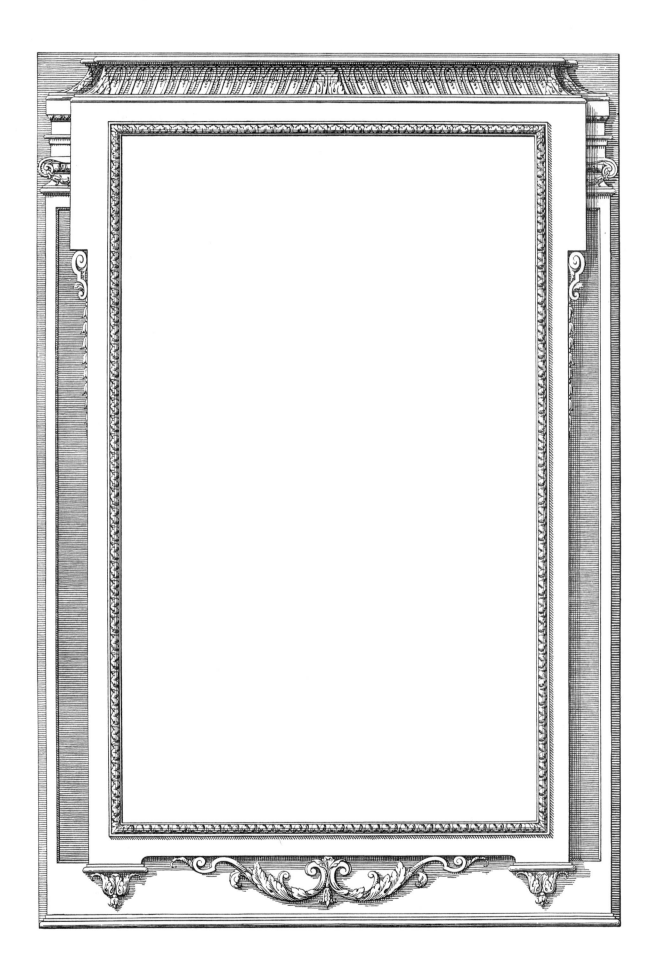

T. M. CLELAND, *1916*

T. M. CLELAND, *1912*

60

T. M. Cleland, *1919*

T. M. CLELAND, *1923*

T. M. CLELAND, *1916*

64   T. M. Cleland, *1917*

T. M. CLELAND, *1916*

T. M. CLELAND, *1921*

T. M. CLELAND, *1917*

T. M. Cleland, *1915 (top); 1919 (bottom)*

T. M. Cleland, *1913*

T. M. Cleland, *1917*

72   T. M. CLELAND, *1915*

T. M. CLELAND, *1920*

T. M. CLELAND, *1914 (top); 1916 (bottom)*

T. M. Cleland, *1923 (top); 1925 (bottom)*

T. M. CLELAND, *1917*

T. M. Cleland, *1917*

T. M. CLELAND, *1913*

T. M. Cleland, *1922*

BRUCE ROGERS, *1923*

BRUCE ROGERS, *c. 1923 (top); 1928 (bottom)*

BRUCE ROGERS, *1924*

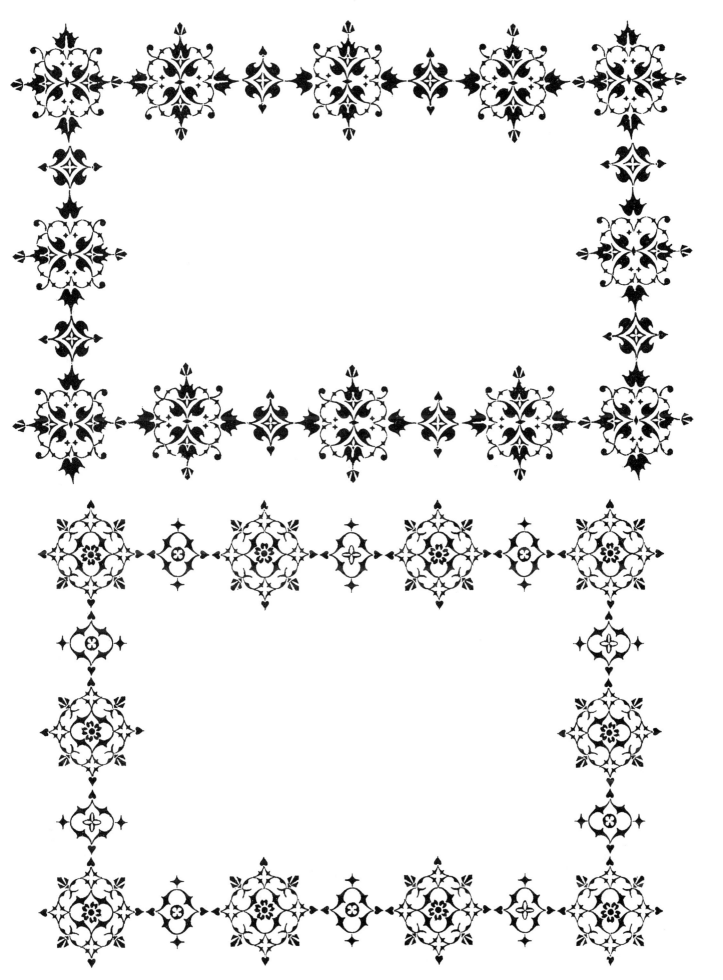

Bruce Rogers, *1930*

BRUCE ROGERS, *1933 (after Fra Luca De Pacioli)*

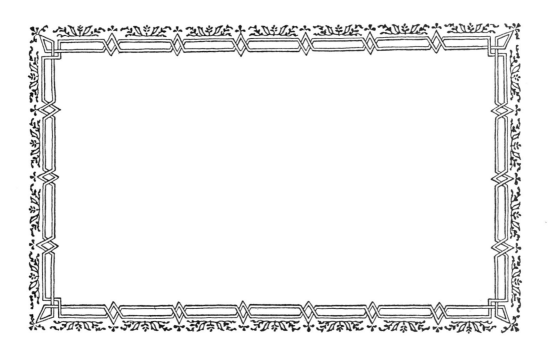

BRUCE ROGERS, *1928 (top); 1909 (bottom)*

90

Bruce Rogers, *1917 (after Albrecht Dürer)*

94   CLARENCE P. HORNUNG, *1926*

96   CLARENCE P. HORNUNG, *1926*

CLARENCE P. HORNUNG, *1927*

CLARENCE P. HORNUNG, *1927*

100

CLARENCE P. HORNUNG, *1923*

CLARENCE P. HORNUNG, *1923*

Clarence P. Hornung, *1922*

CLARENCE P. HORNUNG, *1927*

CLARENCE P. HORNUNG, *1924*

CLARENCE P. HORNUNG, *1924*

CLARENCE P. HORNUNG, *1923*

CLARENCE P. HORNUNG, *1922*

CLARENCE P. HORNUNG, *1921*

CLARENCE P. HORNUNG, *1922*

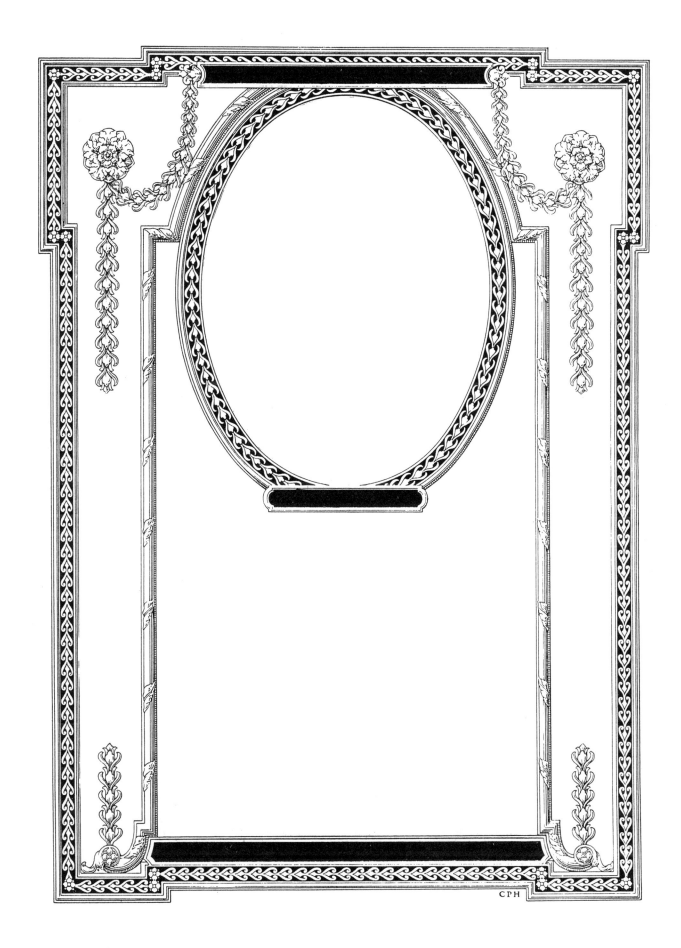

116   CLARENCE P. HORNUNG, *1926*

CLARENCE P. HORNUNG, *1924*

CLARENCE P. HORNUNG, *1922*

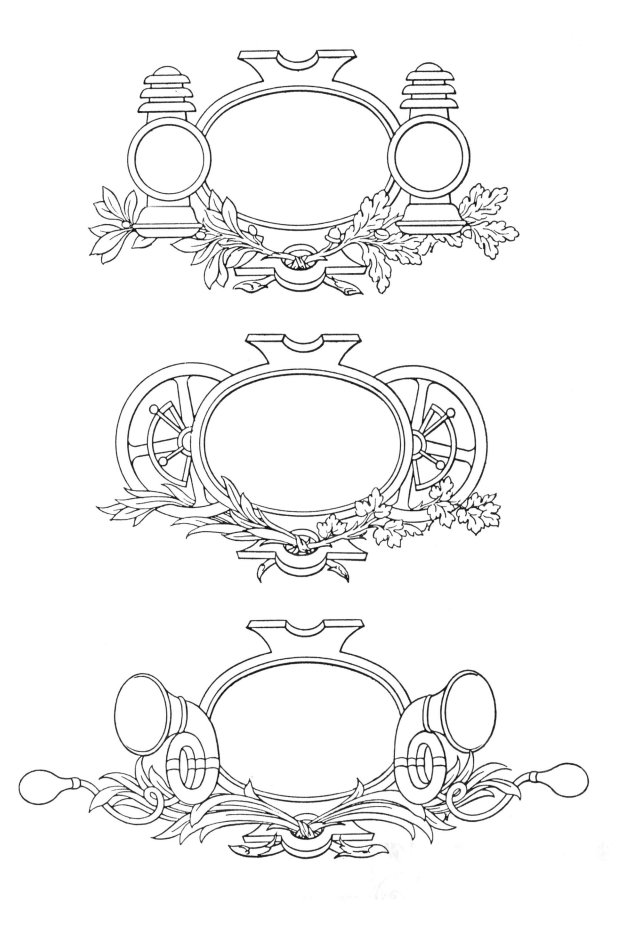

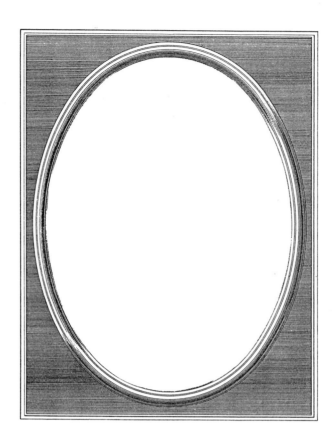
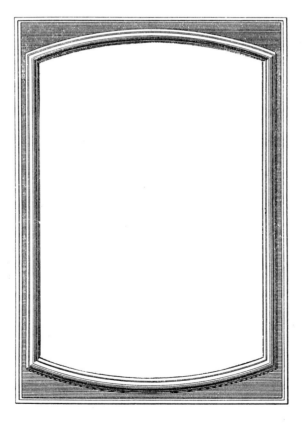
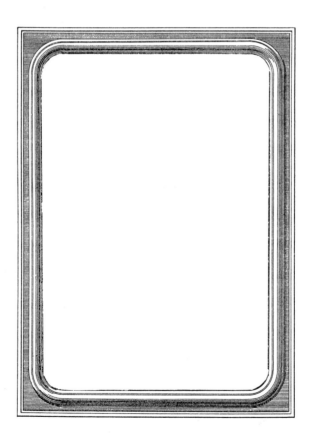

CLARENCE P. HORNUNG, *1925*